PRINCEWILL LAGANG

From Idea to IPO: Navigating the Entrepreneurial Journey

First published by PRINCEWILL LAGANG 2023

Copyright © 2023 by Princewill Lagang

All rights reserved. No part of this publication may be reproduced, stored or transmitted in any form or by any means, electronic, mechanical, photocopying, recording, scanning, or otherwise without written permission from the publisher. It is illegal to copy this book, post it to a website, or distribute it by any other means without permission.

Princewill Lagang asserts the moral right to be identified as the author of this work.

First edition

This book was professionally typeset on Reedsy.
Find out more at reedsy.com

Contents

I   Brief Summary

1	The Genesis of Entrepreneurship	3
2	Idea Generation and Validation	8
3	Crafting Your Business Plan	11
4	Funding Your Venture	15
5	Product Development and Market Entry	19
6	Building Your Brand and Cultivating Customer Loyalty	23
7	The Art of Innovation and Staying Ahead	27
8	Scaling Your Business and Achieving Sustained Growth	31
9	Going Public - The IPO Process	35
10	Beyond the IPO - Challenges and Opportunities	39
11	Navigating the Future - Sustaining Success	42
12	The Legacy and Impact	45

I

Brief Summary

"From Idea to IPO: Navigating the Entrepreneurial Journey" is a comprehensive guide that spans 12 chapters, each covering a significant phase in the entrepreneurial journey. The book takes you through the entire process of starting, building, and sustaining a successful business, culminating in leaving a lasting legacy. Here's a brief summary of each chapter:

1

The Genesis of Entrepreneurship

Title: "From Idea to IPO: Navigating the Entrepreneurial Journey"

In the world of business and innovation, there exists a path less traveled, fraught with challenges and opportunities, and this is the path of the entrepreneur. This journey from idea to IPO (Initial Public Offering) represents the transformation of a mere concept into a thriving, publicly-traded company. The road ahead is neither linear nor easy, but it is a journey that countless visionaries have embarked upon, and in doing so, they have reshaped industries and created a lasting impact on the world. Welcome to "From Idea to IPO: Navigating the Entrepreneurial Journey."

1.1 Introduction

Entrepreneurship is not just about starting a business; it's about changing the world. This chapter is the starting point of your entrepreneurial journey, a journey that will be marked by trials, triumphs, and transformation. In this chapter, we will explore the very essence of entrepreneurship, understanding the driving forces, the characteristics of successful entrepreneurs, and the different stages of development that your idea will go through as you navigate this path.

1.2 The Essence of Entrepreneurship

Entrepreneurship is, at its core, the pursuit of opportunity beyond the resources currently controlled. It's a willingness to take risks, make decisions, and invest time, money, and effort into creating something new or improving upon an existing idea. The entrepreneur is an innovator, a problem-solver, and a visionary. But why do people become entrepreneurs? They do so for a multitude of reasons:

1.2.1 Passion and Purpose
Entrepreneurs are often driven by a passion for a specific product, service, or cause. They see a need or a problem and are determined to provide a solution.

1.2.2 Independence
Many entrepreneurs crave the independence that comes with building and running their own businesses. They want to be their own boss and set their own course.

1.2.3 Opportunity
Identifying opportunities in the market is a key motivator. Entrepreneurs see potential where others see obstacles and are willing to take calculated risks to seize those opportunities.

1.2.4 Wealth and Financial Freedom
The potential for financial rewards and the desire for financial freedom are also strong drivers. Entrepreneurs often see their ventures as a path to financial success.

1.3 The Entrepreneurial Mindset

Successful entrepreneurs possess a unique mindset that sets them apart from others. Some key attributes of this mindset include:

1.3.1 Vision

Entrepreneurs have a clear vision of what they want to achieve. They can see the bigger picture and set long-term goals.

1.3.2 Resilience

The entrepreneurial journey is not without setbacks and failures. Resilience is crucial for bouncing back from challenges and continuing to move forward.

1.3.3 Adaptability

In a constantly changing business environment, adaptability is vital. Entrepreneurs are open to new ideas, willing to pivot when necessary, and able to navigate uncertainty.

1.3.4 Risk-Taking

Entrepreneurs understand the importance of calculated risk. They are willing to take risks when the potential rewards outweigh the downsides.

1.3.5 Creativity

Creativity is a hallmark of entrepreneurship. Entrepreneurs often come up with innovative solutions to problems, creating products or services that stand out.

1.4 The Stages of Entrepreneurial Development

The entrepreneurial journey can be broken down into several stages, each with its unique challenges and opportunities. These stages include:

1.4.1 Idea Generation

At the very beginning, entrepreneurs have an idea that sparks their interest. This idea can come from personal experiences, market research, or a combination of factors.

1.4.2 Feasibility Study

Once an idea is born, it's essential to assess its feasibility. Entrepreneurs need to research the market, competition, and potential risks associated with their concept.

1.4.3 Business Planning

Creating a comprehensive business plan is the next step. This plan outlines the company's vision, mission, strategy, and financial projections.

1.4.4 Funding

To turn the idea into reality, entrepreneurs need funding. They may seek investment from various sources, such as personal savings, loans, venture capital, or angel investors.

1.4.5 Product Development

With funding secured, entrepreneurs can start developing their product or service. This often involves prototyping, testing, and refining the concept.

1.4.6 Market Entry

Bringing the product or service to market is a significant milestone. This stage requires marketing, sales, and distribution strategies.

1.4.7 Growth and Scaling

Once the business gains traction, the focus shifts to growth and scaling. This may involve expanding into new markets, hiring additional staff, and increasing production capacity.

1.4.8 Exit Strategy

The ultimate goal for many entrepreneurs is to reach the stage of an Initial Public Offering (IPO) or another exit strategy, such as a merger or acquisition.

1.5 Conclusion

The entrepreneurial journey is a dynamic and multifaceted endeavor. It requires passion, resilience, adaptability, and a willingness to take calculated risks. In this book, we will explore each stage of this journey in detail, providing you with insights, tools, and guidance to navigate the challenges and make the most of the opportunities that come your way. So, fasten your seatbelt and get ready to embark on a transformative adventure from idea to IPO. Your journey has just begun, and the destination is both challenging and rewarding.

2

Idea Generation and Validation

Title: "From Idea to IPO: Navigating the Entrepreneurial Journey"

In the entrepreneurial journey, the foundation of success is a compelling idea. It's the spark that ignites the entire process, and its quality and viability are crucial to your venture's success. Chapter 2 delves into the critical phase of idea generation and validation, where you transform a concept into a potential business opportunity.

2.1 The Seed of Innovation

Innovation often starts with a single idea, a moment of inspiration, or the recognition of a problem in need of a solution. However, generating a successful business idea isn't just about having a random thought—it's a structured process. Here, we explore various techniques and strategies for idea generation:

2.1.1 Identifying Market Gaps
  Looking for unmet needs or unsolved problems in the market can be a rich source of ideas. Observing consumer frustrations or industry inefficiencies can lead to innovative solutions.

2.1.2 Leveraging Your Expertise

Your unique skills, knowledge, and experiences can serve as a valuable starting point. Your domain expertise can lead to ideas that cater to specific niches.

2.1.3 Brainstorming

Collaborative brainstorming sessions with diverse perspectives can generate a wide range of ideas. Encouraging creativity and removing judgment can yield breakthrough concepts.

2.1.4 Trend Analysis

Keeping an eye on emerging trends, technologies, and consumer behaviors can lead to timely, market-relevant ideas.

2.2 The Importance of Idea Validation

Not all ideas are destined for success, and that's where idea validation becomes critical. You need to test and refine your concept to ensure it has the potential to become a viable business. In this section, we discuss the methods and strategies for idea validation:

2.2.1 Market Research

Conduct comprehensive market research to understand your target audience, competition, and market dynamics. Determine if there's a demand for your idea.

2.2.2 Minimum Viable Product (MVP)

Develop a simplified version of your product or service to test in the market. Gather feedback and iterate based on real-world responses.

2.2.3 Customer Interviews

Engage with potential customers to gather their insights and feedback. This direct interaction can provide valuable information on whether your idea resonates with your target market.

2.2.4 Prototyping

Create prototypes or mockups of your product to visualize and communicate your idea effectively. Prototyping can also help in pitching your concept to potential investors.

2.2.5 Feasibility Assessment

Assess the technical, financial, and operational feasibility of your idea. This step helps you understand the practical challenges and potential roadblocks.

2.3 Case Studies in Idea Generation and Validation

To illustrate the idea generation and validation process in action, we present case studies of successful entrepreneurs who started with a simple concept and brought it to market. We examine their journeys, the challenges they faced, and the strategies they employed to validate their ideas.

2.4 Conclusion

The journey from idea to IPO begins with a single idea, but the success of that idea depends on careful and thorough validation. In this chapter, we've explored the various techniques for generating ideas and the importance of validating those ideas before committing significant resources. In the next chapter, we'll delve into the process of developing a comprehensive business plan to turn your validated idea into a tangible business opportunity.

3

Crafting Your Business Plan

Title: "From Idea to IPO: Navigating the Entrepreneurial Journey"

In Chapter 2, you learned about idea generation and validation, which is the initial phase of your entrepreneurial journey. Now, in Chapter 3, we will focus on the next crucial step: crafting a comprehensive business plan. A well-thought-out business plan serves as the roadmap for your venture, guiding your actions and decisions as you work towards turning your idea into a successful business.

3.1 The Significance of a Business Plan

A business plan is more than just a document for potential investors; it's a tool for entrepreneurs to structure their thoughts, set clear objectives, and anticipate challenges. In this section, we'll discuss why a business plan is essential:

3.1.1 Goal Setting

A business plan helps you define your short-term and long-term goals, creating a roadmap for your company's growth.

3.1.2 Strategic Direction

It outlines your business's strategy, helping you make informed decisions and prioritize your resources.

3.1.3 Communication

A well-prepared business plan can effectively communicate your vision and strategy to potential investors, partners, and employees.

3.1.4 Accountability

It holds you accountable for the goals and milestones you've set for your business.

3.1.5 Flexibility

While it provides a structured framework, a business plan should also allow for adaptability and change as circumstances evolve.

3.2 Components of a Business Plan

A comprehensive business plan typically consists of several key components. In this section, we'll explore these components in detail:

3.2.1 Executive Summary

This section provides a concise overview of your business, highlighting key aspects of your venture, including the problem you're solving, your solution, target market, and financial projections.

3.2.2 Company Description

Here, you describe your company's history, mission, vision, and values. You also define your unique selling points and competitive advantages.

3.2.3 Market Analysis

Analyze your target market, including its size, demographics, trends, and growth potential. Identify your target audience and competition.

3.2.4 Product or Service Description

Detail the products or services you will offer, emphasizing their unique features and benefits. Explain how your offerings address market needs.

3.2.5 Business Strategy

Outline your business strategy, including your pricing, sales, marketing, and distribution plans. Define your sales and revenue model.

3.2.6 Management Team

Introduce your team, their roles, qualifications, and how they contribute to the success of your business.

3.2.7 Financial Projections

Present financial forecasts, including income statements, balance sheets, and cash flow statements. This section is crucial for demonstrating the financial viability of your business.

3.2.8 Funding Requirements

If you need external funding, specify the amount required and how you intend to use it. Explain your fundraising strategy.

3.2.9 Risk Analysis

Identify potential risks and challenges your business may face and detail how you plan to mitigate them.

3.3 Tailoring Your Business Plan

Every business plan is unique, reflecting the specific needs and characteristics of the venture it outlines. We'll discuss strategies for customizing your business plan to suit your specific goals, industry, and audience.

3.4 Case Studies in Business Planning

To illustrate the importance of a well-crafted business plan, we'll examine real-life case studies of successful entrepreneurs who used their plans to secure funding, make strategic decisions, and achieve their business objectives.

3.5 Conclusion

Crafting a business plan is a critical step in transforming your entrepreneurial idea into a successful business. In this chapter, you've learned the essential components of a business plan and its significance in guiding your venture. The next chapter will delve into the crucial aspect of securing funding to support your business's growth and development.

4

Funding Your Venture

Title: "From Idea to IPO: Navigating the Entrepreneurial Journey"

Securing the necessary funding is a pivotal step on the entrepreneurial journey, as it provides the resources required to turn your idea into a thriving business. Chapter 4 delves into the various avenues for funding your venture, from bootstrapping and angel investors to venture capital and crowdfunding.

4.1 The Importance of Funding

Funding is the lifeblood of your entrepreneurial endeavor, enabling you to develop your product, reach your market, and scale your business. In this section, we'll explore the significance of funding in the entrepreneurial journey:

4.1.1 Resource Acquisition
  Funding provides the capital needed to acquire resources, such as talent, technology, and materials.

4.1.2 Market Entry
  It allows you to enter the market, establish your presence, and compete

effectively.

4.1.3 Scaling

With funding, you can expand your operations, increase production, and reach new markets.

4.1.4 Risk Mitigation

Securing adequate funding can mitigate financial risks and provide a cushion during lean periods.

4.2 Funding Options

Entrepreneurs have a range of funding options to choose from, each with its pros and cons. In this section, we'll explore the main sources of funding:

4.2.1 Bootstrapping

Bootstrapping involves using personal savings or revenue generated by the business to fund its growth. We'll discuss the benefits and limitations of this approach.

4.2.2 Friends and Family

Many entrepreneurs turn to friends and family for initial funding. We'll delve into the considerations and potential challenges associated with this source of capital.

4.2.3 Angel Investors

Angel investors are individuals who provide capital in exchange for equity in your business. We'll explore how to attract and engage with angel investors.

4.2.4 Venture Capital

Venture capital firms provide significant funding in exchange for equity. This section will outline the venture capital process and the expectations of venture capitalists.

4.2.5 Crowdfunding

Crowdfunding platforms enable entrepreneurs to raise funds from a broad base of contributors. We'll discuss the various crowdfunding models and strategies for success.

4.2.6 Bank Loans and Lines of Credit

Traditional lending institutions can provide loans and lines of credit to fund your business. We'll explore the application process and considerations.

4.3 Pitching Your Venture

To secure funding, you'll need to effectively pitch your venture to potential investors or lenders. We'll provide guidance on creating a compelling pitch, including how to:

4.3.1 Craft a compelling elevator pitch
    4.3.2 Develop a detailed pitch deck
    4.3.3 Address investor concerns and objections

4.4 Due Diligence and Negotiation

Once you've garnered investor interest, due diligence and negotiation play a critical role in securing a mutually beneficial agreement. We'll discuss the importance of thorough due diligence and provide tips for successful negotiation.

4.5 Case Studies in Funding

To illustrate the funding process in action, we'll present case studies of entrepreneurs who successfully secured funding, highlighting their approaches, challenges, and outcomes.

4.6 Conclusion

Funding your venture is a pivotal step in the entrepreneurial journey, providing the resources required to bring your vision to life. In this chapter, you've learned about various funding options, how to pitch your venture, and the importance of due diligence and negotiation. Chapter 5 will delve into the critical stage of product development and market entry as you work to make your entrepreneurial dreams a reality.

5

Product Development and Market Entry

Title: "From Idea to IPO: Navigating the Entrepreneurial Journey"

In Chapter 5, we dive into the essential phases of product development and market entry, where you transform your idea and initial funding into a tangible product or service and strategically introduce it to your target audience.

5.1 Product Development

Developing your product or service is a pivotal step that demands careful planning and execution. In this section, we'll explore the key aspects of product development:

5.1.1 Ideation to Execution

Transforming your idea into a tangible product requires a detailed plan. We'll discuss the process of refining your concept, creating prototypes, and building a minimum viable product (MVP).

5.1.2 Technology and Tools

Utilizing the right technology and tools can significantly impact the development process. We'll delve into selecting the right software, hardware, and resources.

5.1.3 Team and Talent

Assembling the right team is crucial. We'll discuss how to find and hire the talent you need to bring your product to life.

5.1.4 Project Management

Effective project management is essential for meeting deadlines and staying within budget. We'll explore project management techniques and tools.

5.2 Market Entry Strategies

Once your product or service is developed, the next step is to introduce it to the market. Market entry strategies are vital to ensure a successful launch:

5.2.1 Target Market Selection

Identifying your ideal customer and market segment is the foundation of your market entry strategy. We'll discuss how to define your target market effectively.

5.2.2 Positioning and Branding

Your product's positioning and branding play a significant role in attracting and retaining customers. We'll explore strategies for creating a compelling brand image.

5.2.3 Distribution and Sales

Choosing the right distribution channels and sales strategies can greatly impact your market entry. We'll discuss direct sales, partnerships, and e-commerce options.

5.2.4 Marketing and Promotion

Creating a marketing plan is crucial for reaching your target audience. We'll explore various marketing techniques, including digital marketing, content marketing, and social media.

5.2.5 Competitive Analysis

Understanding your competition is essential for positioning your product effectively. We'll discuss the importance of competitive analysis and how to conduct it.

5.3 Scaling Your Operations

As your product gains traction in the market, you'll need to scale your operations to meet increasing demand. We'll discuss strategies for scaling your business, including:

5.3.1 Expanding Production

Ensuring your production capacity can meet rising demand is critical. We'll explore strategies for increasing production.

5.3.2 Hiring and Team Growth

Scaling often requires hiring additional talent. We'll discuss how to expand your team effectively.

5.3.3 Geographic Expansion

Expanding to new geographic markets is a common scaling strategy. We'll explore the considerations and challenges associated with this approach.

5.4 Case Studies in Product Development and Market Entry

To illustrate the process of product development and market entry, we'll present case studies of entrepreneurs who successfully brought their products to market. These case studies will highlight their strategies, challenges, and achievements.

5.5 Conclusion

The journey from idea to IPO continues with the critical phases of product development and market entry. In this chapter, you've gained insights into the development process and strategies for entering the market successfully. Chapter 6 will explore the importance of building a strong brand and cultivating customer loyalty as you work towards long-term success and growth.

6

Building Your Brand and Cultivating Customer Loyalty

Title: "From Idea to IPO: Navigating the Entrepreneurial Journey"

In Chapter 6, we explore the pivotal role of branding and customer loyalty in your entrepreneurial journey. Building a strong brand and nurturing customer relationships are fundamental to long-term success and growth.

6.1 The Significance of Branding

A brand is not just a logo or a name; it's the personality and identity of your business. In this section, we delve into the importance of branding:

6.1.1 Brand Identity

Define your brand's unique identity, including your mission, vision, values, and personality. Your brand should convey who you are and what you stand for.

6.1.2 Brand Recognition

Creating a distinctive and memorable brand is crucial for standing out in a crowded market. We'll discuss strategies for building brand recognition.

6.1.3 Trust and Credibility

Building trust with your customers is a key component of branding. We'll explore how transparency, consistency, and delivering on promises contribute to trust and credibility.

6.1.4 Differentiation

Your brand should differentiate you from your competitors. We'll discuss how to identify and emphasize what makes your business unique.

6.2 Brand Development Strategies

Developing a strong brand requires a strategic approach. In this section, we'll explore branding strategies, including:

6.2.1 Visual Branding

Your logo, color scheme, and design elements play a significant role in visual branding. We'll discuss how to create a visually appealing brand.

6.2.2 Content Marketing

Content marketing is an effective strategy for conveying your brand's message and connecting with your audience. We'll explore content creation, storytelling, and engagement.

6.2.3 Social Media

Social media platforms provide a powerful avenue for brand promotion. We'll discuss how to leverage social media for branding and customer engagement.

6.2.4 Community Building

Building a community of loyal customers can be a valuable asset. We'll explore strategies for community engagement and management.

6.3 Cultivating Customer Loyalty

Customer loyalty is the bedrock of a successful business. In this section, we'll examine the importance of cultivating loyal customers and strategies for doing so:

6.3.1 Exceptional Customer Service
Delivering exceptional customer service fosters loyalty. We'll discuss how to create a customer-centric culture in your business.

6.3.2 Loyalty Programs
Implementing loyalty programs can incentivize repeat business. We'll explore the design and management of loyalty initiatives.

6.3.3 Feedback and Improvement
Listening to customer feedback and continuously improving your products or services is key to retaining customer loyalty.

6.3.4 Personalization
Personalized marketing and product recommendations can enhance the customer experience and loyalty.

6.4 Case Studies in Branding and Customer Loyalty

To illustrate the importance of branding and customer loyalty, we'll present case studies of entrepreneurs and businesses that have successfully built strong brands and cultivated loyal customer bases. These examples will showcase their strategies and results.

6.5 Conclusion

Building a strong brand and cultivating customer loyalty are essential for long-term success and growth in your entrepreneurial journey. In this chapter, you've gained insights into branding strategies and customer loyalty initiatives. Chapter 7 will focus on the art of innovation and staying ahead in a rapidly changing business landscape.

7

The Art of Innovation and Staying Ahead

Title: "From Idea to IPO: Navigating the Entrepreneurial Journey"

In Chapter 7, we delve into the art of innovation and staying ahead in a rapidly changing business landscape. The ability to adapt, evolve, and innovate is critical for long-term entrepreneurial success.

7.1 The Imperative of Innovation

Innovation is not an option but a necessity in today's dynamic business world. In this section, we'll explore the significance of innovation:

7.1.1 Market Relevance

Innovation is essential for remaining relevant in your industry and meeting the changing needs of your customers.

7.1.2 Competitive Advantage

Innovative products, services, and processes can give your business a competitive edge and differentiation.

7.1.3 Growth and Expansion

Innovation fuels business growth, enabling you to explore new markets, products, and revenue streams.

7.1.4 Resilience

Innovation helps businesses adapt to challenges and disruptions, enhancing their resilience.

7.2 Cultivating a Culture of Innovation

Fostering a culture of innovation within your organization is the first step in promoting continuous creativity and adaptability. We'll discuss strategies for cultivating such a culture, including:

7.2.1 Leadership

Leaders must encourage and support innovation. We'll explore leadership's role in promoting a culture of creativity.

7.2.2 Risk-Taking

Innovation often involves risk. We'll discuss how to create an environment where calculated risks are encouraged and rewarded.

7.2.3 Collaboration

Collaboration and cross-functional teams can stimulate innovative ideas. We'll explore strategies for collaboration.

7.2.4 Continuous Learning

A commitment to continuous learning and skill development is essential for fostering an innovative culture.

7.3 The Innovation Process

Innovation is a structured process that can be managed and nurtured. We'll explore the innovation process, including:

7.3.1 Idea Generation

How to generate and capture innovative ideas from various sources, including employees, customers, and partners.

7.3.2 Idea Screening

Evaluating and prioritizing ideas to determine their feasibility and alignment with your business objectives.

7.3.3 Development and Testing

Taking promising ideas through the development phase, including prototyping and testing.

7.3.4 Implementation

Bringing innovative solutions to market, whether they are new products, services, or internal process improvements.

7.4 Staying Ahead in a Changing Landscape

Staying ahead requires constant vigilance and adaptation. We'll discuss strategies for staying ahead in a rapidly changing business landscape, including:

7.4.1 Environmental Scanning

Monitoring industry trends, competitive moves, and emerging technologies to stay informed and prepared.

7.4.2 Customer Feedback

Listening to and acting on customer feedback to understand their evolving needs.

7.4.3 Agile Business Practices

Adopting agile practices and processes to enhance flexibility and responsiveness.

7.4.4 Investment in Research and Development
Dedicating resources to research and development to drive innovation.

7.5 Case Studies in Innovation and Staying Ahead

To illustrate the importance of innovation and staying ahead, we'll present case studies of entrepreneurs and businesses that have successfully embraced innovation and adapted to changing landscapes. These examples will highlight their strategies and outcomes.

7.6 Conclusion

Innovation is the lifeblood of entrepreneurship, and staying ahead is the key to long-term success. In this chapter, you've gained insights into fostering a culture of innovation, managing the innovation process, and strategies for staying ahead. Chapter 8 will explore the complexities of scaling your business and achieving sustained growth as you journey toward your IPO.

8

Scaling Your Business and Achieving Sustained Growth

Title: "From Idea to IPO: Navigating the Entrepreneurial Journey"

In Chapter 8, we explore the complexities of scaling your business and achieving sustained growth as you work toward your IPO. Scaling is a transformative phase that demands careful planning, efficient execution, and strategic decision-making.

8.1 The Importance of Scaling

Scaling your business is more than just increasing your size; it's about achieving efficient, sustainable growth. In this section, we'll explore the significance of scaling:

8.1.1 Efficient Resource Utilization
Scaling allows you to optimize your resource allocation, improving productivity and profitability.

8.1.2 Increased Market Reach
Expanding your operations enables you to reach new markets and customer

segments, increasing your potential for revenue.

8.1.3 Competitive Advantage
Scaling can provide you with a competitive edge, as larger operations often have cost advantages and a broader customer base.

8.1.4 Attracting Investors
Growth is an attractive prospect for investors, making it easier to secure funding or proceed with an IPO.

8.2 Strategies for Scaling Your Business

Scaling your business involves careful planning, effective execution, and strategic decision-making. We'll explore strategies for successful scaling, including:

8.2.1 Scalable Systems and Processes
Developing systems and processes that can handle increased demands efficiently is essential for scaling.

8.2.2 Financial Management
Effective financial management is crucial for scaling. We'll discuss budgeting, cash flow management, and securing additional funding.

8.2.3 Team Growth and Development
Scaling often involves hiring more employees. We'll explore strategies for recruiting, training, and retaining talent.

8.2.4 Geographic Expansion
Expanding into new geographic markets is a common scaling strategy. We'll discuss the considerations and challenges associated with this approach.

8.3 Overcoming Scaling Challenges

Scaling your business is not without its challenges. We'll explore common scaling challenges and strategies for overcoming them, including:

8.3.1 Operational Efficiency

Streamlining operations and ensuring they can handle increased volume.

8.3.2 Quality Control

Maintaining product or service quality as you scale is crucial for customer satisfaction.

8.3.3 Culture and Leadership

Preserving your company's culture and leadership effectiveness during growth.

8.3.4 Market Saturation

Managing the balance between reaching new markets and saturating existing ones.

8.4 Preparing for an IPO

If your goal is to go public and have an IPO, preparation is essential. We'll discuss the steps involved in preparing for an IPO, including:

8.4.1 Financial Reporting and Auditing

Ensuring your financial statements are accurate and audit-ready.

8.4.2 Legal and Regulatory Compliance

Navigating the complex regulatory landscape and meeting the legal requirements for an IPO.

8.4.3 Investor Relations

Developing relationships with investors and presenting your business in a compelling manner.

8.5 Case Studies in Scaling and Achieving Sustained Growth

To illustrate the complexities of scaling a business and achieving sustained growth, we'll present case studies of entrepreneurs and businesses that successfully navigated the scaling process. These examples will highlight their strategies and outcomes.

8.6 Conclusion

Scaling your business and achieving sustained growth are critical steps on the path to an IPO. In this chapter, you've gained insights into strategies for scaling, overcoming scaling challenges, and preparing for an IPO. Chapter 9 will explore the process of going public and the challenges and opportunities it presents on your entrepreneurial journey.

9

Going Public - The IPO Process

Title: "From Idea to IPO: Navigating the Entrepreneurial Journey"

In Chapter 9, we delve into the process of taking your private company public through an Initial Public Offering (IPO). Going public is a significant milestone in your entrepreneurial journey, offering opportunities for growth, capital infusion, and increased visibility.

9.1 The Decision to Go Public

Going public is a strategic decision that impacts your company's ownership structure, financial reporting, and compliance requirements. In this section, we explore the factors that influence the decision to go public:

9.1.1 Access to Capital
An IPO can provide a substantial influx of capital, which can be used for expansion, debt reduction, and investment in the business.

9.1.2 Liquidity and Exit Strategy
For early investors and founders, an IPO can offer an exit strategy by allowing them to sell shares in the public market.

9.1.3 Brand Visibility

Becoming a publicly traded company can enhance your brand's visibility and credibility.

9.1.4 Regulatory and Reporting Obligations

Going public involves complying with a range of regulatory requirements, including financial reporting, disclosure, and governance.

9.2 Preparing for an IPO

The IPO process is complex and requires thorough preparation. We'll discuss the key steps and considerations for preparing your company for an IPO:

9.2.1 Financial Readiness

Ensuring your financial statements are accurate, compliant, and thoroughly audited is crucial for the IPO process.

9.2.2 Legal and Regulatory Compliance

Navigating the regulatory landscape and ensuring legal compliance, including addressing any potential legal issues.

9.2.3 Investor Relations

Building relationships with potential investors and communicating your business's value proposition effectively.

9.2.4 Board and Governance

Developing a strong corporate governance structure, which is important for public company transparency and accountability.

9.3 The IPO Process

The IPO process involves multiple stages, from selecting underwriters to pricing the shares and making your company public. We'll explore the steps involved in the IPO process, including:

9.3.1 Selecting Underwriters
Choosing investment banks to underwrite your IPO and guide you through the process.

9.3.2 Registration and SEC Filings
Preparing and filing the required registration documents with the Securities and Exchange Commission (SEC).

9.3.3 Roadshow and Marketing
Presenting your business to potential investors through a roadshow and marketing efforts to generate interest.

9.3.4 Pricing and Going Public
Determining the IPO price, issuing shares to the public, and becoming a publicly traded company.

9.4 Life as a Public Company

Becoming a public company entails ongoing compliance, reporting, and governance responsibilities. We'll discuss the challenges and opportunities of life as a public company, including:

9.4.1 Financial Reporting
Regularly reporting financial results and maintaining transparency.

9.4.2 Shareholder Relations
Managing relationships with shareholders and investor communication.

9.4.3 Stock Performance
Monitoring and managing your stock's performance in the public market.

9.4.4 Mergers and Acquisitions

Considering the potential for mergers, acquisitions, or divestitures as a public company.

9.5 Case Studies in IPOs

To illustrate the IPO process, we'll present case studies of companies that successfully went public, highlighting their strategies, challenges, and outcomes.

9.6 Conclusion

Taking your private company public through an IPO is a transformative step in your entrepreneurial journey. In this chapter, you've gained insights into the decision to go public, preparing for an IPO, the IPO process, and life as a public company. Chapter 10 will explore the future beyond the IPO, including post-IPO challenges and opportunities.

10

Beyond the IPO - Challenges and Opportunities

Title: "From Idea to IPO: Navigating the Entrepreneurial Journey"

In Chapter 10, we explore the journey beyond the Initial Public Offering (IPO) and the challenges and opportunities that await entrepreneurs and their companies in the public markets.

10.1 The Post-IPO Transition

After successfully completing an IPO, your company undergoes a significant transition. In this section, we'll explore the post-IPO landscape and its implications:

10.1.1 Public Scrutiny

As a publicly traded company, you are subject to increased public and investor scrutiny.

10.1.2 Shareholder Expectations

Managing shareholder expectations and delivering on promises made during the IPO process is crucial.

10.1.3 Quarterly Reporting

The requirement for regular, detailed financial reporting, including quarterly earnings reports.

10.1.4 Regulatory Compliance

Ongoing compliance with a complex regulatory framework, including the Sarbanes-Oxley Act.

10.2 Post-IPO Challenges

Going public brings its own set of challenges that require careful management. We'll explore some common post-IPO challenges and strategies for addressing them, including:

10.2.1 Stock Price Volatility

Dealing with stock price fluctuations and market volatility.

10.2.2 Investor Relations

Maintaining effective relationships with shareholders and managing investor expectations.

10.2.3 Financial Reporting

Meeting the rigorous demands of quarterly financial reporting and the scrutiny of analysts and investors.

10.2.4 Corporate Governance

Ensuring strong corporate governance practices to maintain transparency and accountability.

10.3 Growth and Expansion

The resources gained from an IPO can be used to fuel further growth and expansion. We'll discuss strategies for using the capital raised in the IPO to expand your business, enter new markets, and pursue acquisitions.

10.4 Innovating and Staying Competitive

Remaining competitive in a dynamic business environment is crucial. We'll explore strategies for innovation and adaptation, including mergers and acquisitions, strategic partnerships, and staying ahead in your industry.

10.5 Case Studies in Post-IPO Success

To illustrate the journey beyond the IPO, we'll present case studies of companies that successfully navigated the post-IPO landscape, highlighting their strategies, challenges, and achievements.

10.6 Conclusion

The journey from idea to IPO is a transformative one, and the challenges and opportunities continue well beyond the public offering. In this final chapter, you've gained insights into the post-IPO landscape and the strategies for managing the challenges and seizing the opportunities that arise in the life of a publicly traded company. The entrepreneurial journey is a dynamic and ever-evolving one, and your ability to adapt, innovate, and persevere will ultimately determine your long-term success.

11

Navigating the Future - Sustaining Success

Title: "From Idea to IPO: Navigating the Entrepreneurial Journey"

Chapter 11 marks the final leg of your entrepreneurial journey as you work to sustain the success you've achieved from the idea stage to becoming a publicly traded company. We'll explore strategies for maintaining growth, fostering innovation, and addressing challenges as your business matures.

11.1 The Long-Term Perspective

Sustaining success in the business world requires a long-term perspective. We'll discuss the importance of setting and pursuing long-term goals and strategies.

11.2 Strategic Growth and Diversification

To sustain success, you must continue to grow and adapt. We'll explore strategies for strategic growth, including product diversification, geographic expansion, and market penetration.

11.3 Innovation and Adaptation

Innovation and adaptation are key to staying competitive. We'll discuss how to foster a culture of continuous innovation and how to adapt to industry changes and emerging technologies.

11.4 Risk Management

Managing risk is crucial to sustaining success. We'll explore strategies for identifying, assessing, and mitigating risks that could impact your business.

11.5 Corporate Responsibility and Sustainability

Incorporating corporate social responsibility and sustainability practices can enhance your business's reputation and long-term viability. We'll discuss the importance of these practices.

11.6 Leadership and Team Development

Strong leadership and an effective team are essential to sustaining success. We'll explore strategies for leadership development and team-building.

11.7 Case Studies in Sustaining Success

To illustrate the journey of sustaining success, we'll present case studies of businesses and entrepreneurs that have successfully navigated the challenges and opportunities of long-term growth and sustainability.

11.8 Conclusion

The entrepreneurial journey is not just about reaching the destination but also about navigating the future and sustaining success. In this final chapter, you've gained insights into the strategies and approaches that will help you thrive as you continue your entrepreneurial adventure. Remember that success is a journey, not a destination, and the possibilities for growth and impact are limitless.

12

The Legacy and Impact

Title: "From Idea to IPO: Navigating the Entrepreneurial Journey"

Chapter 12 marks the culmination of your entrepreneurial journey, where you reflect on the legacy you've built and the impact you've had on your industry, community, and beyond. This chapter explores how to leave a lasting legacy, the responsibilities that come with success, and the opportunities to give back.

12.1 Building a Lasting Legacy

Creating a lasting legacy involves more than just financial success; it's about leaving a positive and enduring impact. We'll discuss strategies for building a legacy that extends beyond your business.

12.2 Corporate Social Responsibility

Businesses today are increasingly expected to be socially responsible. We'll explore the role of corporate social responsibility (CSR) and how your company can contribute to social and environmental causes.

12.3 Giving Back and Philanthropy

As a successful entrepreneur, you have the opportunity to give back to the community and causes you care about. We'll discuss strategies for philanthropy and the impact it can have.

12.4 Mentorship and Entrepreneurial Ecosystem

Mentoring the next generation of entrepreneurs and contributing to the entrepreneurial ecosystem can be a powerful way to leave a lasting impact. We'll explore the benefits of mentorship and ecosystem support.

12.5 Balancing Success with Well-Being

Success often comes with stress and burnout. We'll discuss the importance of balancing your professional achievements with your well-being, including physical and mental health.

12.6 Legacy Planning

Planning for the future and the eventual transition of your business is a crucial aspect of building a lasting legacy. We'll explore strategies for legacy planning and ensuring the continuity of your business.

12.7 Reflections on Your Entrepreneurial Journey

In this final chapter, take a moment to reflect on your entire entrepreneurial journey. Consider the challenges you've overcome, the successes you've achieved, and the lessons you've learned. Reflect on the impact you've had and the legacy you aspire to leave behind.

12.8 Conclusion

Your entrepreneurial journey has been a remarkable one, filled with challenges, triumphs, and personal growth. As you contemplate your legacy

THE LEGACY AND IMPACT

and impact, remember that your journey continues, and there are endless opportunities to make a positive difference in the world. Congratulations on your entrepreneurial success, and may your legacy endure for generations to come.

"From Idea to IPO: Navigating the Entrepreneurial Journey" is a comprehensive guide that spans 12 chapters, each covering a significant phase in the entrepreneurial journey. The book takes you through the entire process of starting, building, and sustaining a successful business, culminating in leaving a lasting legacy. Here's a brief summary of each chapter:

1. Chapter 1: From Idea to IPO: This chapter introduces the entrepreneurial journey, emphasizing the importance of turning an idea into a viable business.

2. Chapter 2: Entrepreneurial Ideation: It explores the process of generating and validating business ideas, laying the foundation for your entrepreneurial venture.

3. Chapter 3: Crafting Your Business Plan: This chapter details the components of a comprehensive business plan, guiding you in structuring your thoughts and goals.

4. Chapter 4: Funding Your Venture: It delves into the various funding options available to entrepreneurs, including bootstrapping, angel investors, venture capital, and more.

5. Chapter 5: Product Development and Market Entry: This chapter focuses on the critical phases of product development and market entry, emphasizing strategies for bringing your product to the market.

6. Chapter 6: Building Your Brand and Cultivating Customer Loyalty: It discusses the importance of branding and customer loyalty in long-term business success.

7. Chapter 7: The Art of Innovation and Staying Ahead: It explores the significance of innovation and adaptability, guiding you on how to foster a culture of innovation and stay competitive.

8. Chapter 8: Scaling Your Business and Achieving Sustained Growth: This chapter details strategies for scaling your business, addressing challenges, and preparing for an IPO.

9. Chapter 9: Going Public - The IPO Process: It outlines the process of taking your company public through an Initial Public Offering (IPO).

10. Chapter 10: Beyond the IPO - Challenges and Opportunities: This chapter discusses life after the IPO, focusing on sustaining success, innovation, and growth.

11. Chapter 11: Navigating the Future - Sustaining Success: It explores strategies for long-term growth, innovation, risk management, and corporate social responsibility.

12. Chapter 12: The Legacy and Impact: The final chapter reflects on building a lasting legacy, corporate social responsibility, giving back, and legacy planning.

Throughout the book, there are case studies, insights, and practical advice to help you navigate your entrepreneurial journey, from idea conception to leaving a lasting legacy. It emphasizes not only financial success but also the positive impact entrepreneurs can have on society and the world.

www.ingramcontent.com/pod-product-compliance
Lightning Source LLC
LaVergne TN
LVHW012129070526
838202LV00056B/5927